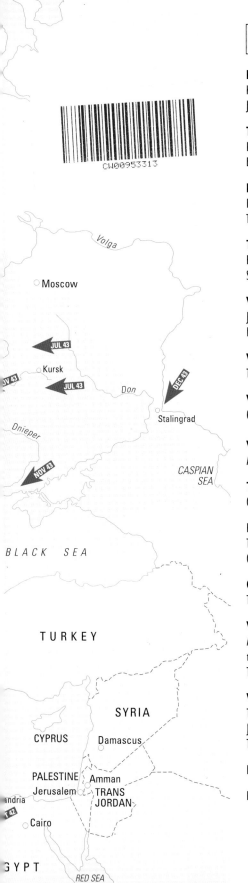

THE SECOND WORLD WAR – CONTENTS

LEFT: The Nazi campaign against Jewish-owned businesses started as early as 1933, reaching a climax with Kristallnacht in 1938.

RIGHT: A triumphant Hitler returns the salute of Austrian admirers in Vienna.

BELOW: British Prime Minister Neville Chamberlain, escorted by Nazi Foreign Minister Joachim von Ribbentrop, leaves Munich on 29 September 1938. He believed he had negotiated an agreement that meant 'peace in our time'.

When the First World War came to a close in November 1918, the victors were concerned to enforce a peace that would last. The Treaty of Versailles, devised mainly by Britain, France and the USA and signed on 28 June 1919, was doomed to fail. It held Germany responsible for the war, and imposed the payment of heavy reparations as well as the loss of territory in the west to Belgium and the return of Alsace Lorraine to France. The treaty also recreated Poland, established the new state of Czechoslovakia from parts of Austria and Hungary, and Hungarian territory again contributed to the new kingdom of Yugoslavia. Germany and Turkey lost their overseas territories which became mandates of the new League of Nations, the international body created to maintain the peace of the world.

The deficiencies of the treaty were not long hidden. The shattered German economy was pinned down by the burden of debt and runaway inflation. Coupled with the wounds to national pride, this undermined the infant democracy, while German-

speaking people who now found themselves citizens of other countries resented separation from the Fatherland. The Italians, although amongst the victors of the First World War, felt poorly rewarded for their

RIGHT: First blood – Japanese soldiers take Manchuria in 1931.

efforts and flocked to the support of the fascist leader Mussolini. Finally, the great economic depression of the 1930s threw millions out of work, all of them eager to lay the blame on others.

Adolph Hitler, born in Austria in 1889, had served in the German army and was both a victim and an exploiter of the peace. He preached the superiority of the 'Aryan' race over all others, particularly the Slavs, whom he equated with all Communists, and the Jews. He blamed the Jews as conspiratorial creators of all Germany's problems. Hitler's National Socialist, or Nazi, party came to power in January 1933 and the pursuit of rearmament and other public expenditure reinforced their popularity; jobs were created. Jewish business premises were vandalized and Jews dismissed from positions of power.

In Italy Mussolini was following similar grandiose, nationalistic designs. Already ruler of Libya, he extended his African domains in 1935 with the invasion of Abyssinia (now Ethiopia) without any effective action by the League of Nations. The anti-democratic aims of both Hitler and Mussolini were confirmed with the creation of the alliance of the Berlin–Rome Axis and from 1936, German support of Fascist rebels in Spain gave their airforce, the Luftwaffe, invaluable combat experience.

France and Britain, fearful of another war and distracted by their own economic problems, did little to resist Hitler's acquisition of territory. He took over Austria, and was welcomed, in March 1938 and at Munich in September persuaded Britain and France to accept the annexation of the German-speaking Sudetenland area of Czechoslovakia. The hope of appeasement buying a permanent peace was shattered six months later when Germany invaded the rest of that country.

In the Far East, also, militarist expansion was threatening world peace. Japan lacked the natural resources to supply a growing industrial economy and was building an empire to gain access to them. Manchuria was invaded in 1931, and China in 1937. An alliance with Germany against Russia, the Anti-Comintern Pact, was made in 1936. The dark shadows of fascism and militarism were spreading remorselessly across the world.

4   The Lights Go Out

With the invasion of Czechoslovakia in March 1939, all hope of peace died. The enclave of East Prussia was separated from the rest of Germany by the Danzig corridor, which gave Poland access to the Baltic Sea. Within a month Hitler had taken from Lithuania the strip of coast projecting north from East Prussia in order to acquire the port of Memel while Mussolini seized command of the Adriatic Sea by taking Albania.

The Allies, Britain and France, were finally forced into action by the signing of the Pact of Steel between Germany and Italy on 22 May. Rearmament was ordered, far too late, and worthless guarantees were given to Poland, Greece and Romania for their territorial integrity.

The next German demand was the return of the Danzig corridor, seemingly a demand too many, but then Hitler pulled a master stroke. In August a non-aggression pact was signed with his erstwhile enemy, the Soviet Union. On 1 September Poland was invaded. The Allies' ultimatum was ignored, and two days later they declared war on Germany.

In practice there was nothing the Allies could do to save Poland and the Germans swallowed up half the country while the Russians took over the rest.

The first action against the Allies was at sea. In preparation for the inevitable conflict, the Germans had begun the deployment of their forces on 19 August when thirty-one submarines, U-boats, put to sea to take up operational positions off the shores of Britain. A week later the pocket battleships *Deutschland* and *Admiral Graf Spee* were on their way to the North and South Atlantic respectively. On 3 September the liner *Athenia* fell victim to a U-boat, the first of many in Germany's campaign to deny supplies to the Allies.

All the pocket battleships were purpose-built, faster than true battleships and, with 11-inch guns, bigger than a cruiser. Their task was to destroy shipping far from Europe, and *Graf Spee* claimed her first sinking on 30 September. To sink the raider, the British had not only to find her, but to assemble overwhelming force against her. The British force, under Commodore Harwood, consisted of the cruisers *Exeter*, *Ajax* and *Achilles* and the heavy cruiser *Cumberland*. Guessing that the *Graf Spee* would be

keen to disrupt the supplies from Argentina, Harwood positioned the three smaller vessels off the River Plate and held the larger in the Falklands. He was right. On the morning of 13 December action was joined, but the heavy guns of the *Graf Spee* soon put *Exeter* out of the fight and the two lighter cruisers shadowed their adversary into the port of Montevideo. Diplomatic delays

ABOVE: ADMIRAL GRAF SPEE outside Montevideo, Paraguay, blown up by the Germans to avoid what they foresaw as certain defeat at the hands of non-existent British reinforcements.

ABOVE: The invading Germans throw a pontoon bridge over a Polish river. Their thorough mechanization enabled them to pursue a strategy of Blitzkreig, lightning war, moving too fast for their adversaries to regroup and resist.

ABOVE RIGHT: April 1939 – Italian cycle troops of the Bersaglieri land at Durazzo, Albania, to reinforce their comrades in the capital, Tirana. The villa of the deposed King Zog stands on the skyline.

about the use of a neutral port, shortage of ammunition and the apparent approach of a huge British force suggested by the fake radio signals he intercepted convinced Captain Langsdorff he was trapped. He left harbour at 18.15 hours on 17 December and at 19.56 the *Graf Spee* was scuttled.

In Europe nothing was happening. This was the time of the Phoney War which lasted for six months; recruits were trained, gas masks were issued, air-raid shelters were constructed.

An ominous quiet persisted as the Allies awaited Hitler's next act.

The Leaders of the Allies

Winston Churchill (1874–1965) seated left. After an undistinguished school career, Churchill became a soldier, and served in India and the Sudan. He entered politics in 1900 and held various ministerial posts between 1910 and 1929, but was then out of power for ten years, continually warning against the rising threat of Nazi Germany. He became Prime Minister of Great Britain in 1940.

Franklin Delano Roosevelt (1882–1945) centre. Roosevelt served as Woodrow Wilson's Assistant Secretary of the Navy from 1913 to 1920, but suffered paralysis of the legs from polio in 1921. Nonetheless he became 32nd President of the USA in 1933, and introduced the "New Deal" to combat the Depression in the 1930s. Re-elected in 1936 and 1940, he turned away from isolationist policies to support resistance to Hitler before the Japanese attack brought America into the conflict.

Stalin; Joseph Vissarionovich Dzhugashvili (1879–1953) right. Became a Bolshevik in 1903 and

adopted the name Stalin (Man of Steel) from 1913. After Lenin's death in 1924 he acquired power by any means possible and, as he controlled the Communist Party, was a virtual dictator from 1927 onwards, responsible for uncounted deaths in various purges of his colleagues and countrymen. In 1941, when Germany invaded Russia, he became Premier and Russia joined the Allies.

6   Blitzkrieg in the West

The next blow fell on Denmark and Norway, the former soon overrun, and the latter the victim of an audacious but costly sea-borne campaign striking at six ports on 10 April. The Allies counter-attacked at Narvik in the far north, expelling the Germans by 13 April and opening the way to an expeditionary force of British and French troops. With the Norwegians they had taken the town by 28 May. But German domination of the air and the advance of her land forces forced the evacuation of the Allies within days.

One of the survivors of the First World War horror of Verdun was Sergeant André Maginot. So impressed was he by the inability of the Germans to break through the fortifications there that, as the French Minister of War, he devoted vast funds to fortifications along the border with Germany. The defence of the northern border was left to the Belgians, neutral in 1940. Neutrality was not a status respected by Hitler, and on 10 May he invaded the Netherlands and Belgium, simply out-flanking the useless Maginot Line.

The British forces in the region, nine divisions under General Gort, had already been weakened by sending assistance north to the Danes and Norwegians, but it was the French, with 72 divisions, who were intended to shoulder the main task. The Seventh Army (seven divisions) were to push forward into Belgium with the British, if the Germans attacked from that direction, to establish a line east of Antwerp and Brussels. Fatally, General Gamelin left his centre weak, and 43 divisions tucked up behind the Maginot Line. The German Panzer (armoured tank) divisions broke through the Ardennes in south Belgium to cut off the forces in the Low Countries, take out their air support bases and advance towards the Channel.

ABOVE: A Heinkel III over London's Docklands. The West India Docks cut across the top of the Isle of Dogs and, south of the Thames in the right corner, is the Royal Naval College at Greenwich.

TOP LEFT: Victorious German troops march down the Champs Élysées, Paris.

LEFT: British troops wade to a rescue ship at Dunkirk.

RIGHT: High Holborn, London, 8 October 1940. Vapour trails of fighters streak the sky.

Boulogne fell on 22 May, Calais by 27 May and the Allied troops were surrounded, apparently doomed, at Dunkirk.

The land there was low and cut by numerous canals and drainage ditches. It was poor country for tank operations and gave the defenders some chance of holding off the German advance. Operation DYNAMO was designed to evacuate some 45,000 men from the beachhead using small boats, pleasure steamers, fishing boats and even yachts, to ferry soldiers across the shallows to the larger vessels in the face of unrelenting raids by the German airforce, the Luftwaffe. By 3 June more than seven times that number, 338,226 men in all, had been rescued, abandoning their equipment, but ready to fight another day.

Paris was occupied, without a fight, on 4 June and France surrendered 18 days later. Two-thirds of the country was occupied and the remaining third was governed by the pro-German Vichy régime. But French defiance was not at an end, for General Charles de Gaulle had escaped to England on 17 June to lead the troops outside France, the Free French.

On 18 June, Winston Churchill addressed Parliament, saying, '. . . the Battle of France is over. I expect that the Battle of Britain is about to begin.' Now only the conquest of Britain remained before Hitler had complete success in Western Europe. While frantic preparations to resist invading forces proceeded, attack from the air started, but fortunately not until 10 July. The British had a small but swiftly growing fighter arm with Spitfire and Hurricane aircraft and, crucially, extensive radar to warn of impending sorties by the Luftwaffe. At first the fighters and their airfields were the principal targets of the bombers, but the RAF refused to crack and frustration led the Germans to switch their attention to London in September. The results were fearful for the Londoners, but the respite permitted the RAF to gain the upper hand. Operation SEALION, the German invasion, was postponed three times before, in the autumn, it was shelved. 503 Allied airmen had lost their lives, and German casualties numbered 3,089. Churchill paid tribute to the victors in the famous words: 'Never in the field of human conflict was so much owed by so many to so few.'

8   The Eastern Front

LEFT: The citizens of Moscow were mobilized to dig defences against the German advance, although this log-and-ditch tank-trap would have stood small chance against the Panzers.

RIGHT: Russian troops in the ruins of Stalingrad, February 1943.

In November 1939 Russia had invaded Finland. Fearing to antagonize Russia, Britain and France left the tiny Finnish army to oppose the Soviets unaided. It took four months for the massive but inefficient Russian force to overcome an enemy with less than half their strength, encouraging Hitler to underestimate Soviet potential.

In June 1941, with the war in the west stalled, Hitler activated the long-planned Operation BARBAROSSA against Russia, ignoring his non-aggression pact with Stalin. In the north, assisted by the Finns, the Germans were besieging Leningrad by September; thousands starved to death before the winter freeze permitted lorry-borne supplies to cross Lake Ladoga. In spite of the huge forces ranged against them, the Russians held on.

Resistance in the south, from Kiev to the shores of the Black Sea, was also tougher than anticipated, forcing Hitler to divert Panzers from the main thrust towards Moscow. By October, when the push towards the capital resumed, the rains had come and the tanks and trucks got bogged down. Next came the snow, and all forward movement ceased for the Germans. An operation planned for completion by the end of the summer had not been backed by the issue of winter clothing, and the invaders suffered accordingly. The Russians, on the other hand, were in their element, infiltrating German lines to harry the enemy and pushing them back from Moscow. By 31 December BARBAROSSA had cost the Germans an unsustainable 1,073,066 casualties, a quarter of them fatal.

Soviet strength was building. The factories that had been removed entire to the east came into production to supply tanks and ammunition. The flow of material from the west that was to persist throughout the war commenced by way of vulnerable and courageous Arctic convoys to Murmansk. Four million tons were dispatched from the USA and the UK from 1941 to 1945, and 300,000 tons were destroyed by enemy action in the hostile waters of the Arctic.

It was Hitler's need for oil that motivated his great strike to the south in June 1942, but his desire also to take Stalingrad, Stalin's city, led him to divide his forces and the swift advance in the Caucasus was halted and, indeed, thrown back. By the time the Germans were outside Stalingrad at the end of August, the Russians had been able to re-inforce the city and a fearful war of attrition ensued. The Germans entered the city in September, but did not reach the banks of the River Volga on which Stalingrad stands until mid-October; four weeks of house-to-house fighting to advance two kilometres! The north of the city still held.

German supply lines were over-extended, and vulnerable from both north and south. On 19 November the Russians counter-attacked, surrounding the Germans at Stalingrad. Attempts to supply them from the air failed, and in December a relief force was brought to a halt 50 kilometres from the city. By 2 February the Germans were finally forced to surrender. They had lost 100,000 in combat, and 90,000 became prisoners, of whom only 6,000 survived the war. Stalingrad itself was a ruin, but it became a symbol for the Russian's stubborn defiance and self-sacrifice.

West of Stalingrad, and due south of Moscow, the Russian advance of the winter had left a salient around Kursk, projecting westwards into German-held territory; a

RIGHT: 'General Winter', Russia's constant ally, impedes the manoeuvrability of the German war machine.

BELOW: Russians unfortunate enough to be overrun by the Germans were slaughtered in their thousands. This scene of grief at Kerch was immortalized by photographer Dmitri Baltermans.

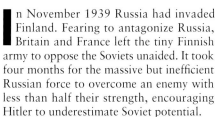

tempting target which Hitler attacked in July 1943.

He was expected. The Soviet defence in depth absorbed the first ferocity of the assault on the northern flank, costing the Germans 25,000 men and 400 tanks and aircraft. On the southern flank initial success brought the Fourth Panzer Army face to face with Soviet T-34 tanks in the biggest tank action the world has ever known, and by 20 July the Germans were being thrown back. Two million men, 6,000 tanks and 4,000 aircraft fought the Battle of Kursk, the last aggressive initiative of the Germans on the Eastern Front.

From here on it was retreat – costly to the Russians, but it was a German retreat all the same.

10   War in the Pacific

In response to the Japanese invasion of China the Americans imposed a trade embargo. This increased the pressure on Japan for expansion to acquire raw materials. But before the rubber of Malaya or the oil of the Dutch East Indies could be seized, the Americans had to be neutralized. They were present in force in their dependency, the Philippines with its deposits of iron ore, copper and other minerals, and the US Pacific Fleet was based at Pearl Harbor in the Hawaiian Islands. Although President Roosevelt had done everything possible, while America was still technically neutral, to supply the Allies in Europe, his country was still not at war and intended to avoid it. This was to change abruptly.

In early December 1941 radio traffic amongst the Japanese became intense. Clearly something was afoot, but the day-to-day routine in Hawaii continued unchanged. At dawn on the same day (although the International Date Line causes it to be recorded as 8 December in East Asia and 7 December in Hawaii) the Japanese attacked the Philippines, Hong Kong, Malaya and Pearl Harbor. At the Hawaiian base, the raiders were seen on radar at 7am, but nothing was done. An hour later the torpedo bombers were amongst the US fleet. It is also possible that a Japanese midget submarine managed to penetrate the protective nets to attack the battleships within. Five of the eight battleships were hit by the first wave and the American aircraft were caught on the ground. By the time the second wave came in the defenders had rallied, and the Japanese losses, five torpedo-bombers, fifteen dive-bombers and nine fighters, discouraged a third wave which might well have completed the destruction. The news of what was dubbed 'the day of infamy' shook America to the core, and war was declared on both Japan and Germany.

Hong Kong was defended by a woefully small British force. Although they were stubborn in resistance, they finally lost control of the vital reservoirs and surrendered on 25 December. The landings on the north-eastern shores of Malaya were resisted only at Kota Bharu, and the British battleship *Prince*

ABOVE: Pearl Harbor, December 1941. The upperworks of the US battleships WEST VIRGINIA and TENNESSEE project above the shallow waters of the harbour amid the smoke of destruction.

LEFT: The skill of the Japanese in jungle warfare persuaded the British that they faced a force far greater than actually existed. The rubber trees in this plantation were to provide essential raw materials for the Japanese empire.

TOP LEFT: Japanese landing parties charge into Hong Kong.

BELOW: The Japanese premier, General Hideki Tojo, salutes the guard of honour on his visit to the Philippines on 5 May 1943. On his right is General Waji, Director-General of the Japanese Government of Occupation.

of *Wales* and the battlecruiser *Repulse*, sent to counter-attack, were sunk by Japanese aircraft, demonstrating the absolute necessity to command the skies. The Indian, Australian and British troops were steadily and swiftly forced south as the Japanese demonstrated their skill in the jungle and plantations of the Malay peninsula. By 31 January 1942 the British had withdrawn to Singapore, where the mighty guns installed for the protection of the vital seaport could only be trained to bear on attackers from the sea. On 15 February Singapore surrendered.

Air power was also the key to the conquest of the Philippines. The Japanese attack on Clark Field, the US airbase, destroyed most of the aircraft on the ground and within two days the American airforce had ceased to be a significant factor in the campaign. The main Japanese landings took place on 22 December, but it was not until 9 April 1942 that the Americans were forced to surrender, and the island of Corregidor held out until 6 May.

The Dutch East Indies campaign started on 11 January 1942, and the islands of Borneo, Sumatra, Java and Timor fell successively until, by early March, the Japanese conquest was complete. The Japanese advance into Burma began on 20 January and was equally remorseless. Rangoon fell on 8 March and, with troops now available from conquered Malaya, the Japanese pushed the ill-assorted British, Indian, Burmese and Chinese defenders back to the border with India by mid May.

In six months Japan had extended its domination to all of East Asia and threatened Australia to the south and India to the west. It was not until May that they met with their first check. In an attempt to isolate Australia from the Americans, they sent forces to New Guinea and a fleet into the Coral Sea, north-east of the Australian coast. Admiral Nimitz, C-in-C of the US Pacific Fleet countered their move and an ill-defined sea battle followed, in which both sides had major difficulty in finding their enemies at all. Losses on both sides were considerable; the US had two aircraft carriers, *Yorktown* and *Lexington*, put out of action for the time being, and the Japanese lost the battle in the air. But the invasion of New Guinea failed, and, for the first time the advance of Japan had been stemmed.

Although it is convenient to consider the fighting on land, sea and in the air as separate activities, it must not be forgotten that the co-ordination of the three was usually the key to success, most notably in the final invasion of Europe by the Allies. Weapons and machinery developed to levels of sophistication that often outran the ability of the commanders to use them to the full, but at the same time the great mass of movement was by means centuries old. Occupation of the ground and the defeat of the enemy's armies in the field remained essential, and this involved the 'poor bloody infantry' slogging ahead on foot, and supplies following somehow; the horse and cart played a key role even in such dashing operations as BARBAROSSA in Russia.

On land the great innovation of the previous war, the tank, achieved new heights of power and sophistication, but the way to use it was not clear. Some saw it as a sort of free-ranging metal horse, rushing about wreaking mayhem on the opponent's infantry, others as a mobile gun emplacement working in support of infantry attacks. It could be either, both or neither, depending on terrain and circumstances. In Blitzkrieg, 'lightning war', working with motorized infantry, the tank was a formidable weapon, and the open country of North Africa or the great plains of Russia also gave it the scope to act virtually independently – as long as not threatened from the air, and as long as it had superior gun-power. The major faults of the British tank were its feeble gun and light armour. In Normandy the principal Allied battle tank was the American-built Sherman. Light, fast, mech-

anically reliable and with a greater turret traverse speed than its opposition, it was also under-gunned and with such a propensity to burn when hit it was nick-named the 'tommy cooker'. The German Panther carried a gun of sufficient muzzle-velocity to penetrate 138mm of armour at 90 metres and was protected by 100mm of frontal armour and 45mm of side armour, while the heavier, slower Tiger had similar firepower and 80mm of side armour. The Sherman had 76mm of front armour and a gun capable of penetrating 74mm of armour at 90 metres. The refusal of the chiefs to recognise these deficiencies cost lives and also morale; the men knew they had inferior machines. Possibly the finest tank of the war was the Russian T-34 with its 76.2mm gun.

Against the tank, the British had the

ABOVE: At Houfalize in the Ardennes, a Tiger tank stands as a memorial in the main street.

LEFT: A German tank destroyer with a 75mm gun at the Museum of the Battle of Normandy, Bayeux.

RIGHT: An American Sherman tank outside the Airborne Museum, Ste-Mère-Eglise, France.

PIAT which hurled a bomb 135 metres, too near for confident use, and the Americans the bazooka with an inadequate projectile. The German Panzerfaust could deal with 200mm of armour at 27 metres, close work, but with a power to inspire trust. Guns mounted on tank-like vehicles, tank destroyers, supplemented conventional anti-tank guns, but the greatest advance was the British discarding-sabot round which shed its shell-like outer part after exiting the gun barrel, leaving a hardened steel spike to

penetrate the enemy's armour.

Allied infantry weapons also proved less than satisfactory. Rifles did not get much use in actual battle. Research showed that as few as 15 per cent of riflemen opened fire in a given action. Their precision was irrelevant when the situation called for a saturation of fire. Here the German light machine-guns, known to the Allies as Spandaus, were superb. An MG 42 delivered 1,200 rounds a minute compared to the 500 of a British Bren, and a German infantry company carried sixteen machine-guns compared to the nine of a British or eleven of an American company.

Whatever the power of the weapons, the essential thing was to have enough of them. The huge productive capacity of America, Britain and the Soviet Union could not be matched by that of Germany. The supreme factor, however, was the quality of the command structure and its personnel, and here the Germans had the gravest possible disadvantage, a leader who did not hesitate to countermand his generals and took any criticism of his ideas as treachery.

Even before war was declared German operations to deny sea-borne supplies to Britain started with the deployment of U-boats in the western approaches to the English Channel, the first move in what became known as the Battle of the Atlantic. Once France had fallen and Norway had been taken, the Germans had forward bases from which they could pose a threat to Britain's sea-lanes through the Channel and round the north of Ireland to Liverpool. In addition to submarines, aircraft and mines, the Germans had surface raiders in the shape of fast and heavily armoured battleships approaching readiness for launching.

The experience of the early months of the war confirmed the vital role of the convoy to resist attack, but there was a woeful lack of escort-vessels, balanced, fortunately, by a shortage of U-boats. By mid-1940 Allied shipping losses were mounting. German ability to locate targets was assisted both by their skill in decoding signals and by the arrival of the Focke-Wulf Condor long-range reconnaissance aircraft. 140 Allied ships were sunk in June 1940 and the monthly figures through to December read 105, 92, 100, 103, 97 and 82. In 1941 the Germans adopted the 'wolf-pack' tactic, forming their U-boats into groups that shadowed the convoys and attacked on the surface at night. The co-ordination of such an attack made for heavy radio traffic and eventually the British were able to pin-point this so accurately that the U-boats became targets in their turn. Detection by improved radar supplemented the existing sonar underwater system, and, by the end of 1941, Allied losses had ceased to increase in spite of a tripling of the size of the German U-boat force.

In March 1941 the Lease-Lend Bill was signed in the USA, giving Britain access not only to surplus American destroyers, but also to refitting facilities in US shipyards. New, faster and purpose-built escort vessels were being launched. The Canadian and then the American navies were a growing strength and the aircraft of Coastal Command were flying to protect convoys as far off as Iceland. The fortunes of battle were tipping in favour of the Allies. Finally, the need to supply their armies in North Africa forced the Germans to divert U-boats to the Mediterranean, and with them went the last chance of victory in the Atlantic.

LEFT: The convoy system reduced the number of Allied losses. U-boats had to evade the escort vessels to make a kill.

RIGHT: The daunting fire-power of the battleship BISMARCK accounted for HMS HOOD before air attack in 1941 left her vulnerable to British battleships.

BELOW: HMS BELFAST at her mooring opposite the Tower of London. She was one of the cruisers at the Battle of North Cape in December 1943, when the SCHARNHÖRST was sunk.

LEFT: The British aircraft carriers INDOMITABLE, with a superannuated aircraft taking off, and EAGLE on convoy protection duty heading for Malta. Both took part in the vital PEDESTAL mission in August 1942 to deliver supplies to Malta.

With the recognition of the importance of air-power arose the supremely important role of the aircraft carrier. Particularly in the Pacific, where airfields on tiny islands took too long to build to support the island-hopping campaign, both bombers and fighters were flown off US carriers. In the Pacific battleships still played a major part in the American campaign, but their vulnerability to air attack switched the prime task to the aircraft carrier. In combined operations, with the navy putting troops ashore under an umbrella of aircraft, battleships provided essential covering fire, their huge guns delivering a massive tonnage of explosives.

When Germany's battleship *Tirpitz* was completed, she was stationed in Alten Fjord on the northern tip of Norway, a constant threat to the Arctic convoys. Unsuccessful attempts to sink her were made by 'human torpedoes', torpedo-like devices ridden like motor-bikes and with detachable warheads. Midget submarines, X-craft, with two-ton explosive packs on each side to be dropped under the target on time fuses, attacked in September 1943. Six set off, towed behind conventional submarines, but two failed to complete the crossing. Released 25 miles away from their target, another was soon forced to give up and X5, X6 and X7 were left. X7 and X6 were seen and fired on, but managed to drop their charges, while what became of X5 is not known. *Tirpitz* was moved slightly before the explosion came, and though not fatally damaged, was immobilized for six months. All the X-craft were lost, two with all hands. *Tirpitz* was eventually sunk in 1944 by the 'Tallboy' bombs of the Lancasters of 617 Squadron.

A s the Luftwaffe demonstrated, air power in support of the army was a vital ingredient of the Blitzkrieg. Fighters protected bombers to knock out bridges and disrupt communications, and the much feared Stuka dive-bomber had a devastating and demoralizing effect on troops. With the expulsion of the British from Continental Europe, the conflict entered a rare phase of being exclusively an air war. At the start of the Battle of Britain what was left of Fighter Command after the defeats in France and Norway amounted to some 470 serviceable aircraft, 330 of which were Hawker Hurricanes or Supermarine Spitfires. The sturdy Hurricane was the mainstay of the defence.

German bombers were escorted by protective screens of fighters, but the fast and

RIGHT: The well-armed but cumbersome ME-110.

BELOW: The Stuka dive-bomber added to its physical impact with the fitting of a siren that emitted a fearful shriek as it swooped to the attack.

nimble Messerschmitt 109 had limited range, and often counted its operational time over England in minutes. The two-seater Messerschmitt 110 was a more clumsy craft that was frequently reduced to flying in defensive circles while the bombers were left to face the fighters alone. It was, perhaps, this early experience of a purely aerial battle that convinced the Air Marshals that the war could be won by air power alone, and led to a determination to bomb Germany out of the war rather than to work in close co-operation with forces on land and sea.

The usefulness of aircraft against naval targets lacking air cover was demonstrated by the Japanese, who used Mitsubishi A6M2 Zero fighters, Achi D3A2 Val dive-bombers and Nakajima B5N2 Kate bombers, some carrying torpedoes, against the Americans at Pearl Harbor. British capital ships, likewise, proved easy prey for the Japanese off Malaya. In the long series of island-hopping battles to regain territory from them, the Americans depended heavily on carrier-borne and island-based aircraft, including the Dauntless dive-bomber, the Devastator torpedo bomber and the Wildcat

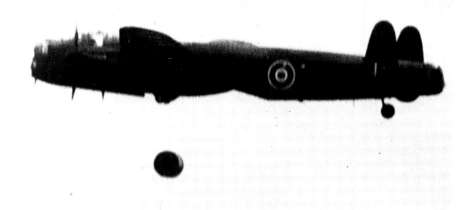

RIGHT: The drum-like form of a dam-buster bouncing bomb leaves the Lancaster's bomb-bay during a training exercise.

LEFT: The American Mustang, one of the finest aircraft of the war.

BELOW: A weapon that transformed the concept of warfare, the V-2 missile.

fighter. In this theatre the B-17 'Flying Fortress', a bomber bristling with defensive gunnery, first gained fame. It was to become the principal daylight bomber over Germany in the European campaign.

The success of the landings in Normandy in 1944 derived to a significant extent from Allied domination of the air. The American P-51 Mustang, once fitted with the Rolls-Royce Merlin engine, proved to be more than a match for its opponents. It was capable of 475 mph, and, with drop tanks, had the range to fly to Berlin and back. The co-ordination of air and ground operations was learnt the hard way. In the early days in Normandy liaison between army and air-force was poor, but by the end of the campaign the Hawker Typhoon, the RAF fighter-bomber capable of carrying eight 50-pound rockets or 2,000 pounds of bombs, was responsible for terrible slaughter amongst the retreating Germans.

Airmen had considerable faith in the usefulness of bombers operating from great heights. However, the morale of neither the British nor the Germans was broken by the blitzing of their towns, and damage to industrial installations, though useful, was not fundamental to victory. The mainstay of the RAF's bomber forces was the Lancaster, and it was in Lancasters that the heaviest conventional bombs were carried. These craft also starred in the raid in May 1943 that destroyed the dams of the Ruhr with Barnes Wallis's incredible bouncing bomb, and in the later raid that, using the 'Tallboy' bomb, sunk the *Tirpitz*.

Too late to turn the tide, the Germans introduced weapons that would change the nature of warfare itself, the flying bombs. The V-1 was a jet–propelled unmanned aircraft, which a Spitfire was just capable of chasing and shooting down, but the V-2 rocket was another matter altogether, and it was very fortunate that the Allied advance of 1944 in Normandy and the Low Countries overran the launching bases before extensive damage could be done.

The Second World War was, more exactly than previous conflicts, total war; no one was non-combatant. Although the 'laws of war' were observed in many respects, it was considered quite legitimate to attack civilian targets, killing women and children, the old and the infirm. In Nazi territory it was also considered desirable to exterminate whole groups of people, Jews, Slavs, gypsies, or to use them as forced labour until they died of exhaustion, starvation or disease, or even to use them in medical experiments.

In the Nazi-occupied countries resistance movements arose to harass the invaders. These were supported by the Allies both in order to gather intelligence and to sabotage industrial installations and communications. Captured by the German secret police, the Gestapo, resistance fighters were often tortured to betray their comrades and then executed. The innocent suffered as well; whole villages were wiped out in reprisal for the successes of the partisans.

LEFT: In November 1940 Coventry was the victim of one of the heaviest German raids of the war. The cathedral, except only the spire, was burnt out and much of the city flattened.

BELOW: The ruins of Dresden, Germany, 1945. In addition to the direct damage from bombs, the city suffered a fire-storm. As bombs fell on the already burning centre, the hot air rising drew in winds from the outskirts, fanning the flames to an incredible heat, consuming the oxygen and suffocating survivors, almost all of them civilians.

In Britain no-one could forget that there was a war. Children were evacuated from the major cities to the safety of the countryside, and those that stayed often passed the night huddled in air-raid shelters or deep in the security of the London Underground. Men too old or unfit for active service became members of the Local Volunteer Force, later the Home Guard – 'Dad's Army'. Jobs left vacant by men who had gone to fight were filled by their wives and girl-friends, both in Britain and America. With food in short supply, gardens were turned over to the growing of vegetables and meat, butter and eggs were rationed. Chocolate, ice-cream and bananas became only a memory. Petrol, clothes, furniture and other goods were rationed too. Not without cause did Britain's leaders wonder how long the people could endure.

LEFT: While an air-raid warning sounds, Londoners of all ages take shelter in the Underground.

BELOW LEFT: Women at work on a bomber fuselage in the USA.

BELOW: As the Allies approached Paris in August 1944, the local resistance fighters and police took up arms against the Germans.

I n April 1941 the German whirlwind swept through Yugoslavia and Greece, and in spite of gallant defence, the Allies were ejected from Crete, falling back to Egypt. The Italians in Libya were retreating before the British, and the Germans began their build-up to reinforce the Axis in February 1941 under General Erwin Rommel. He moved quickly to the east and pushed the small British forces back, isolating the port of Tobruk on the Libyan coast some 60 miles from the Egyptian border, and on into Egypt itself. Tobruk could give the Germans a harbour to bring in supplies from Italy, but to Rommel's anger the defending Australians would not surrender.

Late in 1941 the British retaliated, relieving Tobruk, but with the British in Malta almost neutralized as a threat to German convoys, new strength flowed into Rommel's forces. His surprise attack in January 1942 had the Allies back to a line from Gazala on the coast to Bir Hakeim where the 1st Free French Brigade held stubbornly in spite of being outflanked on 26 May. Short of fuel, the German advance lost momentum but the British counter-attack was delayed until 5 June, and then it failed. The line collapsed, Tobruk fell and the British were back in Egypt.

Crucial to the progress of both sides was the island of Malta. A British naval base, it also provided airfields from which German supply convoys could be attacked. Malta endured months of ferocious attacks from the air.

Rommel, now a Field Marshal, attacked again in late June, pushing the British back to the next possible line of defence, only 60 miles from Alexandria, on a line running south from El Alamein, where the exhaustion of both sides brought a halt. In August 1942 Churchill arrived in Egypt to make changes. General Alexander replaced Auchinleck as the Commander-in-Chief, and General Bernard Montgomery was appointed commander of the Eighth Army. He adopted and improved upon the existing in-depth defensive plan, and Rommel's 30 August attack failed.

Montgomery built his strength, resisting calls from London for immediate action, and restored the morale of his men, training them, visiting them and demonstrating his ability to plan in depth and detail. When the British struck on 24 October they broke the German line, and by 3 November were rolling forward. On 8 November the Americans under General Dwight D. Eisenhower landed in Morocco and the British in Algeria in Operation TORCH. Victory in North Africa was assured, but Rommel's skill made it anything but easy. It was not until May 1943 that the Allies prevailed.

Churchill next persuaded the Allies to attack 'the soft underbelly' of Europe, Italy,

ABOVE: Lt Col David Sterling with a Long Range Desert Group patrol of the unit he founded, the SAS. Operating behind enemy lines, they disrupted the German communications and gathered intelligence.

RIGHT: The ruins of Cassino with the monastery of St Benedict above, the target of the heaviest bombing of the Italian campaign.

LEFT: British Churchill tanks advance at El Alamein.

RIGHT: General Erwin Rommel, the 'Desert Fox', in North Africa. He had distinguished himself in the conquest of France in 1940, and, in Africa, showed himself to be a master of mobile warfare.

rather than undertaking a cross-Channel campaign. It proved to be anything but soft. The US Seventh Army under General George S. Patton and the British Eighth Army under Montgomery landed in Sicily on 10 July 1943 and overcame the Italian and German forces by 17 August. On 24 July Mussolini was ousted from power and the new Italian government started secret negotiations with the Allies. The Germans started to pour reinforcements into Italy.

On 3 September an armistice was signed with the Italians, and the first Allied troops landed on the 'toe' of the Italian mainland on the same day. Six days later the US Fifth Army landed at Salerno, south of Naples and the British First Airborne Division at Taranto, on the 'heel' of Italy. The Americans ran into trouble. The coasts are dominated by the central mountain chain, and from those heights German fire poured down on the beach-head. The landing was reinforced just in time, and the Germans withdrew to the Gustav line, 80 miles south of Rome.

The Allied advance of October was hampered by the onset of winter rains. In January 1944 the strongpoint of Monte Cassino held up progress, and an attempt to outflank the Germans was made at Anzio, but the unopposed landings were not followed up; Cassino had to be taken to relieve Anzio. French and New Zealand troops made costly attacks for no gain, and it was not until May that the Americans and French broke the Gustav line elsewhere, isolating Cassino. Finally, after the town and the historic abbey had been reduced to rubble, Polish troops took the ruins. The Americans entered Rome on 4 June failing to prevent the Germans from escaping.

LEFT: Protected by barrage balloons, landing-craft pour supplies ashore. As the Luftwaffe posed no threat and German guns found the balloons useful ranging markers, they were soon pulled down.

The defeat of Hitler depended, inevitably, on the eventual invasion of France and an advance on Germany. Normandy was selected as the landing area. An elaborate programme of deception convinced the Germans that the Pas de Calais was the target leaving the minimum opposition in Normandy. The western beaches, Utah on the eastern shore of the Cotentin Peninsula and Omaha to the north-west of Bayeux, were allocated to the Americans under Lt General Omar Bradley, while the three beaches to the east, Gold, Juno and Sword, were British and Canadian objectives. Command of the armies was in the hands of General, now Sir, Bernard Montgomery and the Supreme Commander was General Eisenhower.

The preparations were immense. By May 1944, 20 American divisions, 14 British, three Canadian and one each from Poland and France, nearly 8,000 aircraft, 4,000 landing-craft and ships and nearly 300 fighting ships were in readiness – 2,876,439 men in total. But a major problem remained – the weather. Summer gales are common in the English Channel and 1944 was no different. The intended date of D-Day passed in storms, but on the eve of 6 June a break in the weather prompted the order to go.

In the first two hours of the new day airborne troops landed by glider and by parachute on the eastern and western flanks of the front, seizing communication lines and protecting the target beach-heads. At dawn

the huge fleet of invading vessels closed the coast and the landings commenced. At Utah beach resistance was minimal, and to the east it was strong but soon overcome. On Omaha beach it was hell on earth, and the Americans staggered under fire from the Germans, but by evening the Allies were established on the shores of France.

The plan was to drive inland to secure Caen in the east, and then use the Americans to thrust south and create a north-south front which would roll eastwards. The immediate response of the Panzer regiments made Caen unattainable in the short term, and the unexpected problems encountered in the nature of the terrain held up progress everywhere. The bocage – the pattern of little fields and thick hedges so charming to the tourist – offered perfect country for a defensive campaign. The Panther and Tiger tanks of the Panzer regiments were superior to the Allies' machines and the co-ordination of air and land operations was not yet perfected. The arrangements for supplying the liberators, on the other hand, worked well. Huge quantities of stores were landed on the beaches, and a vast artifical 'Mulberry' harbour was constructed at Arromanches. Its remains survive today.

By 17 June the Americans had established themselves astride the Cotentin Peninsula and by the end of the month had taken Cherbourg, but the British were still held up outside Caen. The first week of July saw the effort to advance to the east of the city

ABOVE: The countryside of Normandy is scattered with memorials to the fallen of many nations. Here the characteristic cross and headstones denote the British cemetery at Bayeux, close to the Museum of the Battle of Normandy.

RIGHT: Paratroops spearhead the landings in southern France in August 1944.

BELOW: The ruins of German defences at Pointe du Hoc commemorate the courage of the victorious Americans.

BELOW: Paris is free!

stall and the second, after heavy bombing, the occupation of the northern half of the town. On 18 July an attack round the east of Caen, intended to open the road to Falaise, also failed, although the city itself was taken and the front line was now south of it. Although the breakthrough still evaded Montgomery, the bulk of the German forces were tied down on the eastern flank.

In the west the Americans had been grinding forward through the bocage, and on 18 July took St Lô. On 24 July, following a massive air bombardment, they thrust south once more, and the opposition crumbled. By 30 July Patton was in Avranches with Brittany and the Loire before him and little to stop him taking them. South of Caen the Canadians battled forward together with the Poles and by 16 August the Germans were confined to a salient bounded by Argentan in the south and Falaise in the north – the Falaise pocket. Here the airforce tore into them, destroying men, horses and machines in their hundreds while they struggled to escape to the east. By 21 August half the German army were dead or prisoners, and all their equipment was lost.

There was little resistance as the Allies swept forward. Paris was theirs by 25 August, Brussels by 3 September and by 15 September the front line ran from Antwerp to Aachen on the German border and south beyond Nancy.

On the Eastern Front the Russian advance was inexorable, but was cynically delayed in early August to allow the Germans to wipe out the Polish Underground Army which had risen to take Warsaw. When Soviet troops entered Warsaw three months later they found a ruined city, devoid of any inconvenient democratic alternative to their rule.

LEFT: After the battle, the bridge 'too far' at Arnhem is strewn with the debris of war.

BELOW: The Ardennes offensive. Men of the 2nd Panzer Grenadiers in a schimmwagen, an amphibious VW beetle, pause to orientate themselves in the 'Battle of the Bulge'.

Two physical barriers impeded the Allied advance into Germany. One was artificial, the Siegfried Line or West Wall along the borders of France, Luxembourg, Belgium and part of the Netherlands. It was not, in fact, anything like as strong as the Atlantic Wall in Normandy, but the Allies could not be sure. The other barrier was natural, the river system – the Rhine across Germany and the Netherlands to Rotterdam and the Meuse or Maas passing through Liège and Maastricht, then running north to Nijmegen before turning west to the sea. In southern Belgium were the wooded hills of the Ardennes, scene of the unanticipated German advance of 1940.

In an attempt to secure river crossings and sweep into Germany north of the West Wall, Operation MARKET GARDEN was planned. In September 1944 airborne forces landed at Arnhem and, south of there, Nijmegen, securing the bridges, but the more northerly group was defeated, in spite of determined resistance, before the push from the south could support them. It was in the Vosges mountains towards Strasbourg that the most striking success was achieved, and by 15 December the Americans were on the point of crossing the Rhine.

Hitler's counter-attack, through the Ardennes with the intention of splitting the British and Americans apart and reaching Antwerp, was a complete surprise. On 16 December the last of the German armoured strength dashed forward towards Bastogne, which they surrounded, and on towards Dinant. Snow lay heavy over the hills, and proved to hamper the Germans as much as

their adversaries. The Allies rallied, Bastogne held (German demands to surrender being dismissed with the single word 'Nuts!' by US General McAuliffe), and the Panzers ran short of fuel. Within six weeks the Germans had been thrown back, having squandered much of the strength needed to resist the Russian advance in the east.

The formidable obstacle of the Rhine remained. Preparations to blow the bridges had been made, but, to avoid accidental demolition, the explosives were unprimed. On 7 March 1945 the Americans beat the retreating Germans to the bridge at Remagen, which they took with infantry and tanks immediately after the explosives went off but failed to destroy it. Other crossings followed and by early April the whole east bank was in Allied hands. The advance to

RIGHT: 30 April 1945.
The Soviet flag is raised
over the ruined
Reichstag, the
Parliament building,
in Berlin.

ABOVE: On 3 May 1945
Montgomery repeats the
conditions for peace;
unconditional surrender.

BELOW: Twin towers of
the Ludendorff railway
bridge at Remagen still
stand on the banks of
the Rhine. The bridge
collapsed ten days after
the Americans took it,
killing 28 of the
engineers working on it.

the River Elbe had become irresistible.

In the east Marshal Zhukov with the 1 Belorussian Front and Marshal Konev with the 1 Ukrainian, 2.5 million men and the greatest concentration of gunnery of all the war, were on the River Oder, 40 miles from Berlin, facing one million Germans. On 16 April they attacked, and by 25 April Berlin was surrounded. On the same day the Russians and Americans met on the Elbe. The Germans defended their capital with outstanding tenacity. Hitler killed himself on 30 April and resistance ceased on 2 May.

Early in the morning of 3 May Montgomery's headquarters on Lüneberg Heath was approached by a delegation from Admiral Dönitz, Hitler's successor. Montgomery received them abruptly. 'Who are you? What do you want?', according to his interpreter, Captain Derek Knee. The Germans failed to get any response other than the demand for unconditional surrender, and returned the following day to sign the document. The war in Europe was over, but the scenes discovered as the Allies liberated such camps as Dachau, Buchenwald and Auschwitz revealed a depth of horror that outstripped anything imaginable.

Although checked in the Coral Sea in May 1942, Japan was still advancing, and June showed Midway Island was the objective. The attack was on a massive scale. Admiral Yamomoto used almost all of the Japanese fleet, 162 vessels. But he did not know their signal code had been broken. The US Commander-in-Chief Admiral Nimitz was ready.

The Americans hit hard; aircraft sunk three of the four Japanese carriers and ended the domination of their fleet in the Pacific. Having protected their position in the north, the Americans sought to secure the line in the south, landing Marines on 7 August 1942 on Guadalcanal in the Solomon Islands, east of Papua New Guinea, to protect the link with Australia. In the following months recurrent sea battles imposed fearful losses on both sides, with no conclusive result, while the US Marines created a legend with their heroic stand. The three-day sea battle of Guadalcanal in November was so destructive that the waters are now known as Ironbottom Sound. The two dozen wrecks there include two Japanese battleships; the balance of seapower tilted towards the USA. Island-hopping forward, the Americans took the last of the Solomons in November. Nimitz then commenced clearing the islands between the Solomons

LEFT: Japanese Kamikaze pilots receive their final briefing.

RIGHT: Burma, November 1944. Men of the British 36th Division wade across a river on the advance to Mohnyin.

and Wake Island, 2,000 miles west of Hawaii. He took the Marshalls in January 1944, and pushed stubbornly onwards to reach the Marianas by the middle of the year. Each landing was opposed by dedicated Japanese and each imposed a heavy burden on the attackers.

Far to the west, the British had been attempting to make an impression on the Japanese in Burma, but without success. The myth of Japanese invincibility in jungle warfare was destroyed by the forces under Brigadier Orde Wingate, the Chindits, who operated behind enemy lines. Aware that forces were being assembled for the invasion of Burma, the Japanese carried out a pre-emptive strike at Imphal and Kohima on the Indian border in April 1944. The British and Indians were surrounded but, supplied from the air, continued to resist

until relieved in June. The Japanese retreated, hotly pursued, having lost 65,000 men, their heaviest defeat of the war so far.

General Douglas MacArthur, the US Commander-in-Chief, South-West Pacific, was determined to regain the Philippines and operations commenced in October 1944. The sea battles of Leyte Gulf were the last fought by the Japanese Combined Fleet, and here it was defeated. The fighting reached the principal, northern island, Luzon, in January 1945 and by March 1945 the Americans had all practical control.

The island of Iwo Jima lies halfway between the Mariana Islands and Japan itself. Not only was it part of the Japanese homeland, but also the perfect base for fighter aircraft to escort bomber raids on the Japanese mainland. Only eight square miles in area, it was a single fortress with 22,000 troops. The US Marines landed on 19 February 1945 but it was not until 26 March, having lost nearly 7,000 men and killed almost every Japanese soldier, that they prevailed.

Okinawa, between Japan and Formosa (Taiwan), was invaded on 1 April. This island, less than 70 miles long, was not conquered until 21 June. The US land forces lost

some 7,000 killed and 32,000 wounded, while the navy suffered 10,000 casualties. Over 100,000 defenders died, and over 4,000 suicide pilots, Kamikaze, gave their lives attempting to destroy Allied ships. If this was the price of taking the outlying islands, what would be that of conquering Japan itself?

On 6 August 1945 a new and terrible weapon was unleashed. The first atomic bomb, equivalent to 20,000 tonnes of TNT, was dropped over Hiroshima. 80,000 died at once, and thousands more were to succumb to radiation diseases in time to come. On 9 August a second atomic explosion destroyed Nagasaki. Faced by this horror Japan surrendered.

At last the Second World War, in which 45 million people died, was at an end. The forces of fascism had been defeated, but at terrible cost.

The peace posed new challenges to democratic freedom. Faced with the might of the Communist powers of the USSR and China eight years later, Churchill was to write, 'Only the atomic bomb stretches its sinister shield before us. The danger of a Third World War . . . casts its lurid shadow over the free nations of the world.'

ABOVE: On 14 August 1945, General MacArthur signed to accept Japanese unconditional surrender.

LEFT: Landing-craft carry US Marines shorewards at Iwo Jima.

RIGHT: The ruins of Hiroshima, the first victim of the atomic age.

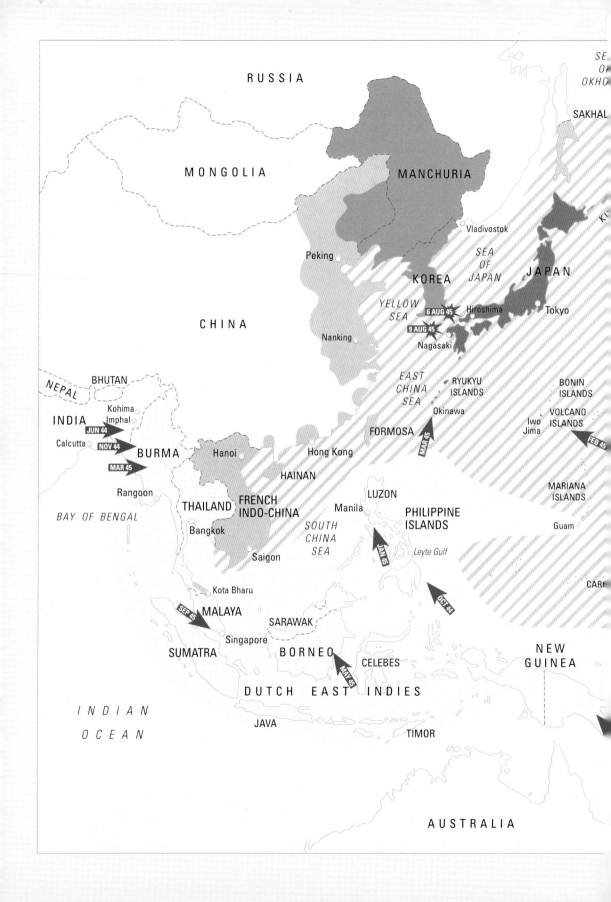

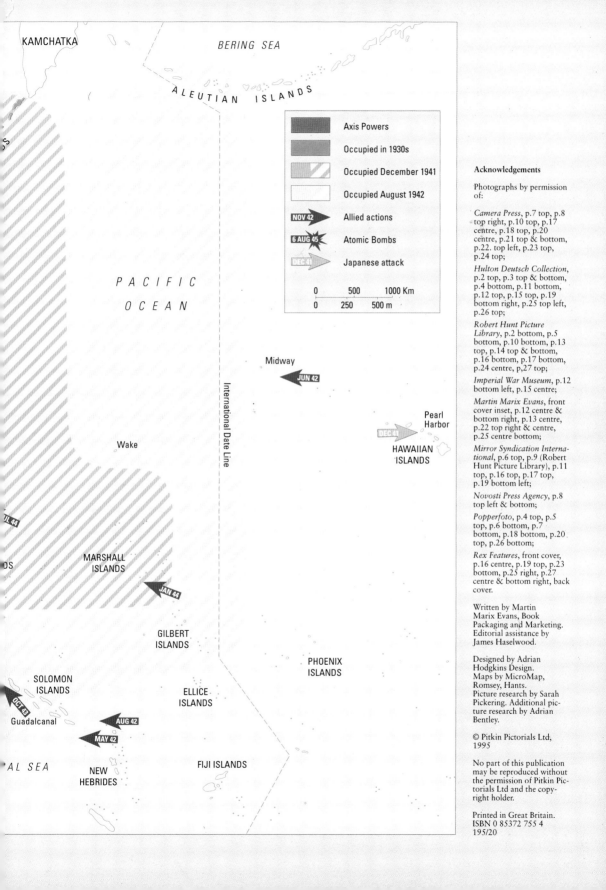

KAMCHATKA

BERING SEA

A L E U T I A N   I S L A N D S

Legend:
- Axis Powers
- Occupied in 1930s
- Occupied December 1941
- Occupied August 1942
- NOV 42 — Allied actions
- 6 AUG 45 — Atomic Bombs
- DEC 41 — Japanese attack

0 — 500 — 1000 Km
0 — 250 — 500 m

P A C I F I C

O C E A N

Midway

JUN 42

International Date Line

Pearl
Harbor

DEC 41

Wake

HAWAIIAN
ISLANDS

JUL 44

MARSHALL
ISLANDS

JAN 44

GILBERT
ISLANDS

PHOENIX
ISLANDS

SOLOMON
ISLANDS

OCT 43

ELLICE
ISLANDS

Guadalcanal

AUG 42

MAY 42

AL SEA

NEW
HEBRIDES

FIJI ISLANDS

Acknowledgements

Photographs by permission of:

Camera Press, p.7 top, p.8 top right, p.10 top, p.17 centre, p.18 top, p.20 centre, p.21 top & bottom, p.22. top left, p.23 top, p.24 top;

Hulton Deutsch Collection, p.2 top, p.3 top & bottom, p.4 bottom, p.11 bottom, p.12 top, p.15 top, p.19 bottom right, p.25 top left, p.26 top;

Robert Hunt Picture Library, p.2 bottom, p.5 bottom, p.10 bottom, p.13 top, p.14 top & bottom, p.16 bottom, p.17 bottom, p.24 centre, p,27 top;

Imperial War Museum, p.12 bottom left, p.15 centre;

Martin Marix Evans, front cover inset, p.12 centre & bottom right, p.13 centre, p.22 top right & centre, p.25 centre bottom;

Mirror Syndication International, p.6 top, p.9 (Robert Hunt Picture Library), p.11 top, p.16 top, p.17 top, p.19 bottom left;

Novosti Press Agency, p.8 top left & bottom;

Popperfoto, p.4 top, p.5 top, p.6 bottom, p.7 bottom, p.18 bottom, p.20 top, p.26 bottom;

Rex Features, front cover, p.16 centre, p.19 top, p.23 bottom, p.25 right, p.27 centre & bottom right, back cover.

Written by Martin Marix Evans, Book Packaging and Marketing. Editorial assistance by James Haselwood.

Designed by Adrian Hodgkins Design. Maps by MicroMap, Romsey, Hants. Picture research by Sarah Pickering. Additional picture research by Adrian Bentley.

© Pitkin Pictorials Ltd, 1995

No part of this publication may be reproduced without the permission of Pitkin Pictorials Ltd and the copyright holder.

Printed in Great Britain. ISBN 0 85372 755 4 195/20

'We shall defend our island, whatever the cost may be, we shall fight on the beaches, we shall fight on the landing grounds, we shall fight in the fields and in the streets, we shall fight in the hills; we shall never surrender.' WINSTON CHURCHILL 4 JUNE 1940

ABOVE: Jews – men, women and children – from the Warsaw ghetto, being rounded up by the Nazis. Their terrible fate was revealed when the Allies liberated the death camps.

FRONT COVER: St Paul's Cathedral in the Blitz 29 December 1940.

There are many sites and museums (some of them are listed below) that evoke the terrible carnage but magnificent spirit of the times – probably none more so than those associated with the D-Day landings in Normandy.

UNITED KINGDOM

Cambridgeshire
Imperial War Museum (Duxford)

Dorset
Tank Museum (Bovington)

Hampshire
Airborne Forces Museum (Aldershot)
Aldershot Military Museum
D-Day Museum (Southsea)
Museum of Army Flying (Middle Wallop)
Royal Marines Museum (Southsea)
Royal Naval Museum (Portsmouth)
Royal Naval Submarine Museum (Gosport)

London
Cabinet War Rooms (Whitehall)

Guards Museum (Wellington Barracks)
HMS Belfast (Pool of London)
Imperial War Museum (Lambeth)
National Army Museum (Chelsea)
National Maritime Museum (Greenwich)
RAF Museum (Hendon)

Merseyside
Maritime Museum (Albert Dock)

Scotland
Scottish United Services Museum (Edinburgh Castle)

Somerset
Fleet Air Arm Museum (Yeovilton)

Sussex
Military Aviation Museum (Tangmere)

FRANCE

Normandy
The Landing Museum (Arromanches)
Museum of the Battle of Normandy (Bayeux)
Memorial, a Museum for Peace (Caen)

Paris
La Musée de l'Armée (Les Invalides)

BELGIUM
Victory Memorial Museum (Arlon)
Bastogne Historical Center (Bastogne)

THE NETHERLANDS
Airborne Museum (Arnhem/Oosterbeek)
Groesbeek Museum (Nijmegen)

Pitkin Guides are available by mail order from: Pitkin Pictorials, Healey House, Dene Road, Andover, Hampshire, SP10 2AA, UK
Tel: 01264 334303
Fax: 01264 334110

 PITKIN

ISBN 0-85372-755-4

9 780853 727552 >